First published in Great Britain in September 2022
Latch Patch Publishing
Shrewsbury
Shropshire

Photographs and design at Latch Patch Publishing

ISBN 9781999376543

I would like to dedicate my books to Phil, my hubby, who has had to put up with me being totally obsessed with my crochet passions for years, including the lockdown years! Sorry!

I would like to thank my sister Kath, for her owl and her two stitch face!

I would like to thank my local group of ladies, the Crochet Newbies, who got me started!

Also Di, for keeping me going! For Devin my lovely cheerleader, and for Bonnie for her amazing crocheted pictures.

Latch Patch Publishing

Projects

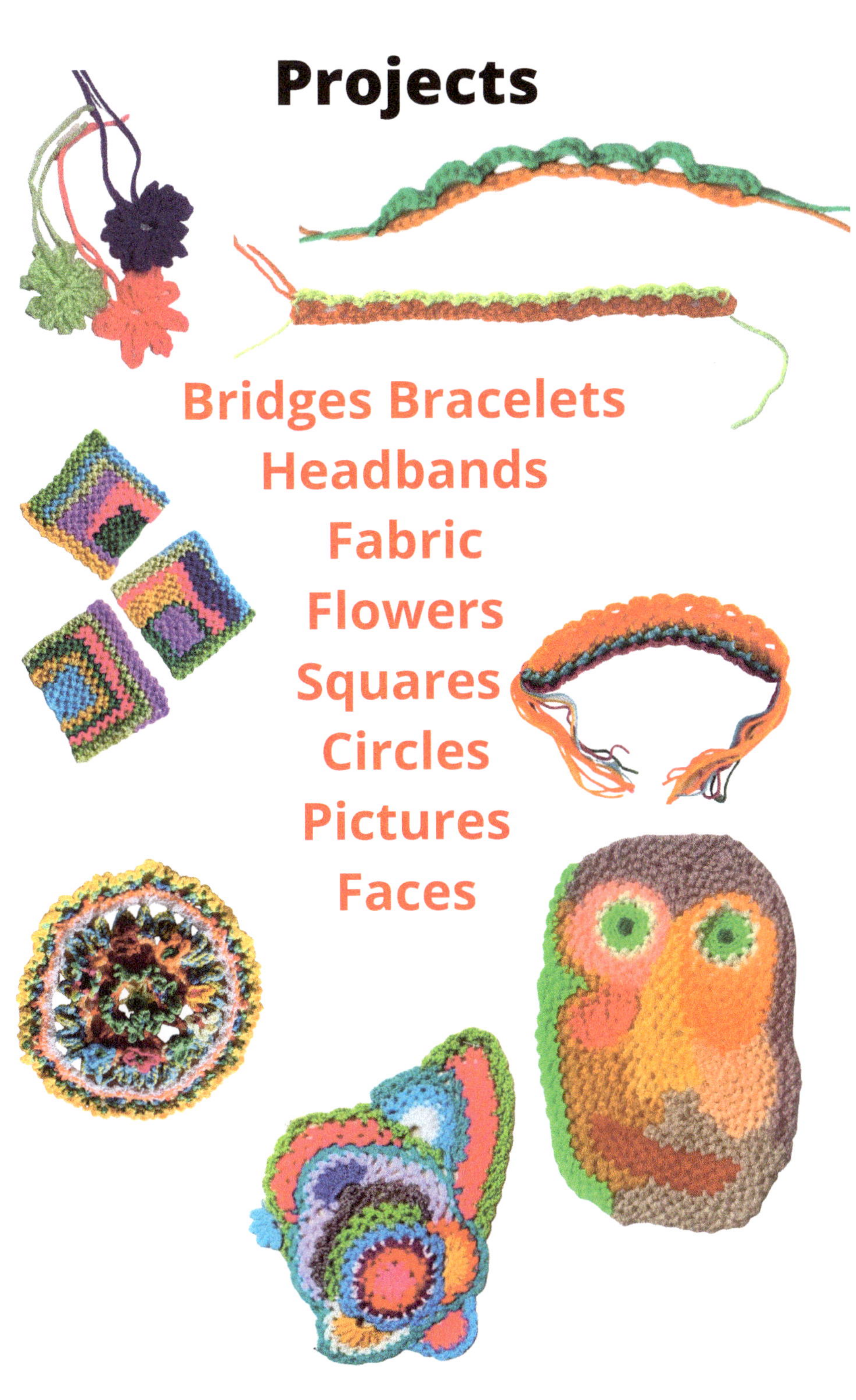

Bridges Bracelets
Headbands
Fabric
Flowers
Squares
Circles
Pictures
Faces

Two Stitch Crochet

This new idea began when looking at possible projects to teach beginners crochet. I soon began to realise, that very few crochet tutors teach this way and that it could be a new and unique method, of creating easy crochet. It is so simple to get started, as it is only necessary to teach two stitches and to learn two stitches.

These two stitches are **chain and slip stitch** and these are combined to make **'bridges'.**

The best way to learn how to use these bridges, is to practice using different sized bridges. *Then,* learn how to increase the number of rows to make a fabric. It is possible to make a fabric or a picture, by making some random patches, that can be worked around.

There are 3 stages to work through

1) Learning how to make the 'bridges bracelets'.
2) Learning how to make the two stitch fabric.
3) Using the two stitch 'bridges method' to create your own art.

- When making your crocheted pictures, you are creating your own design and there is no pattern to follow.
- It is intended to look original and it will evolve as you crochet.
- Once you have learned how to make the crochet bridges, you can use them freely to make patches of fabric.
- Remember, that you can make extra bridges when shaping each element.

Making Bridges

Begin, by learning how to make a chain.
Find my YouTube channel (free to subscribe)
youtube.com/c/RoslynHillLatchHookCrochet
and follow this link.
youtu.be/NCKerR4SDoU
Next, make the two colour bracelet
using the YouTube link.
youtu.be/cdoSGkOtvgc.

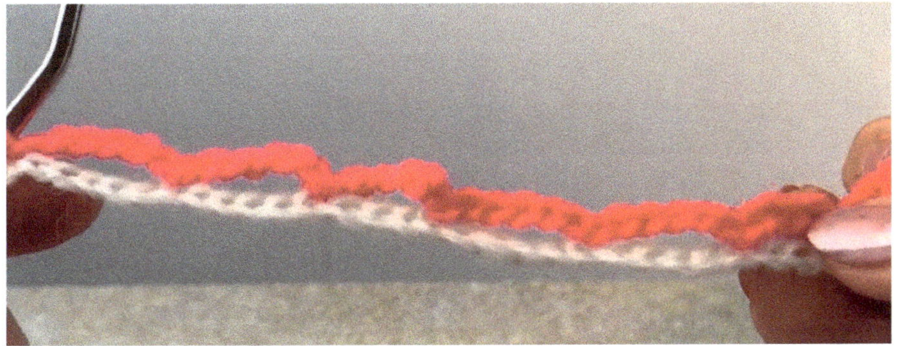

The idea of making bridges, is that we can hook under them easily, to make the slip stitch. The slip stitches of the first row are worked into the foundation chain, but for the second and following rows it gets easier as it is possible to hook under the bridges to make the slip stitch. The bridges (holes) are easy to hook under with the latch hook, although you may use a traditional hook.

Begin with bridges made with 5 or 6 chains. Later, make chains of 4, 3 and even 2, to make a tighter fabric.

The photo above is the two colour bracelet, introduced in book 1. I didn't realise at the time, that this particular bracelet, featuring two colours, would be the idea behind creating a fabric. I now refer to them as 'bridges bracelets'.

Bridges Bracelets

Making lots of these bracelets is recommended, to get used to making chain bridges.

Practice making a variety of chains, using between 2 and 5 chains between the slip stitches.
The less chains there are in each bridge the tighter the fabric.

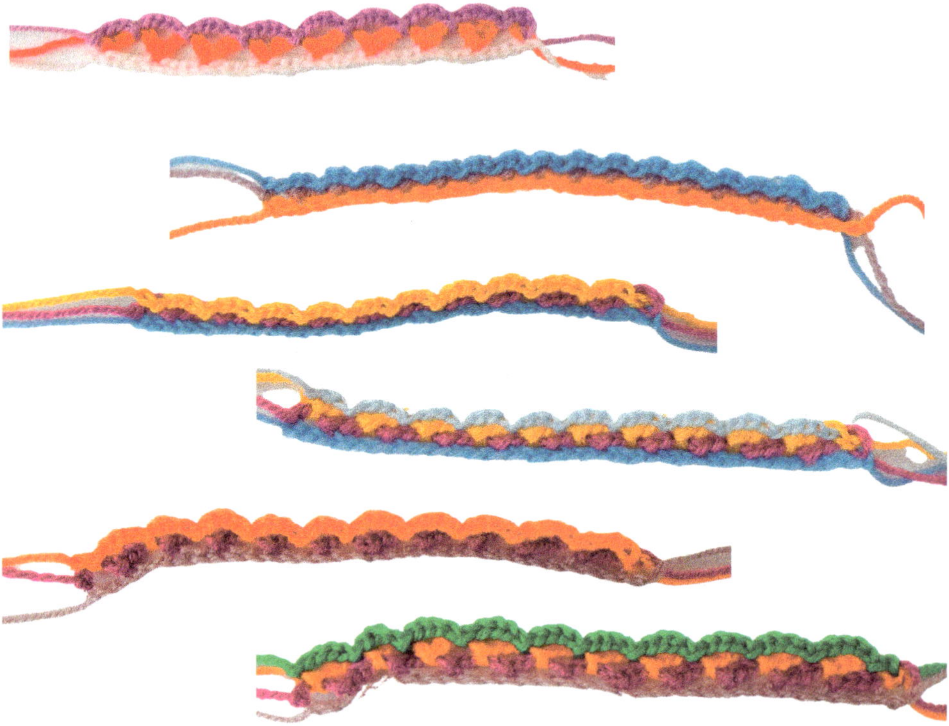

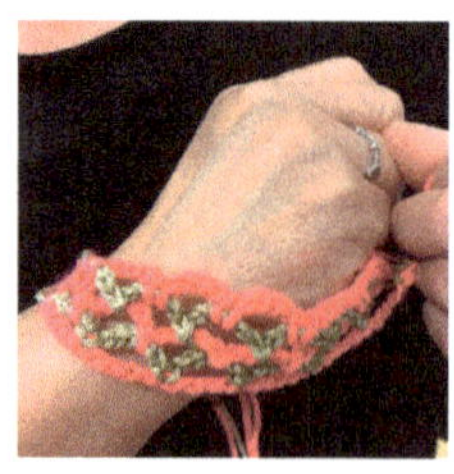

Perhaps, try to make this bracelet first, and make it as wide as you like!

Making a Fabric

Practice getting started by experimenting with bridges.

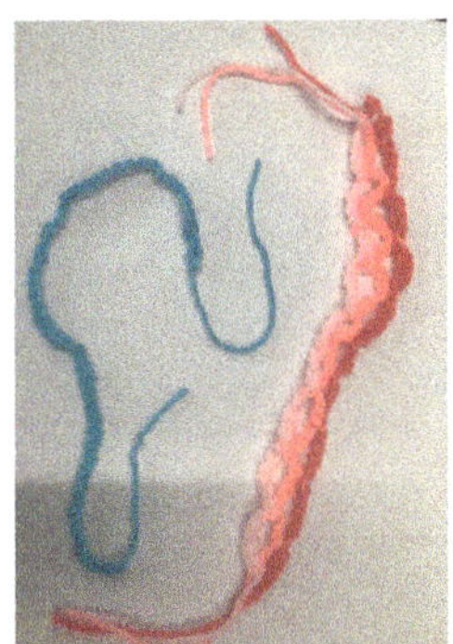
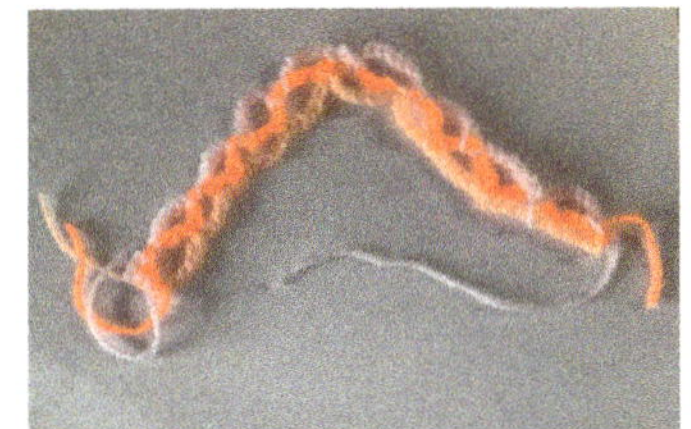
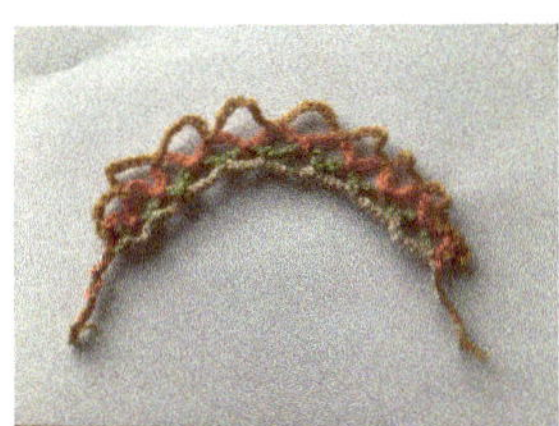
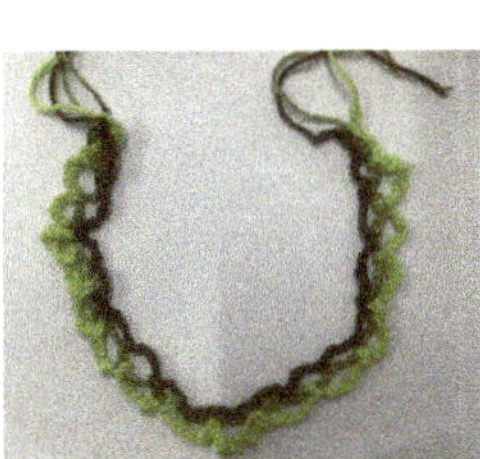
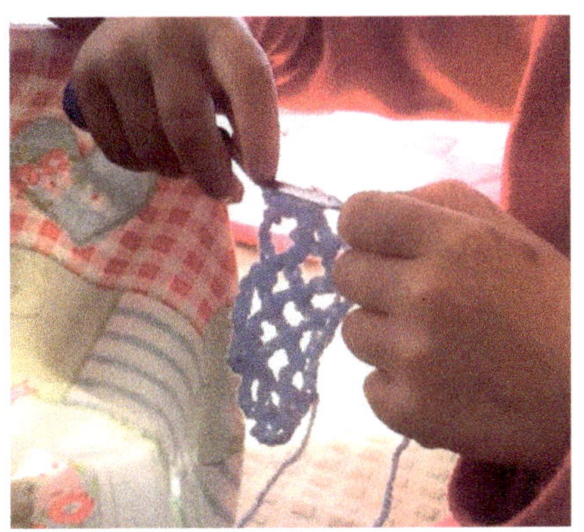
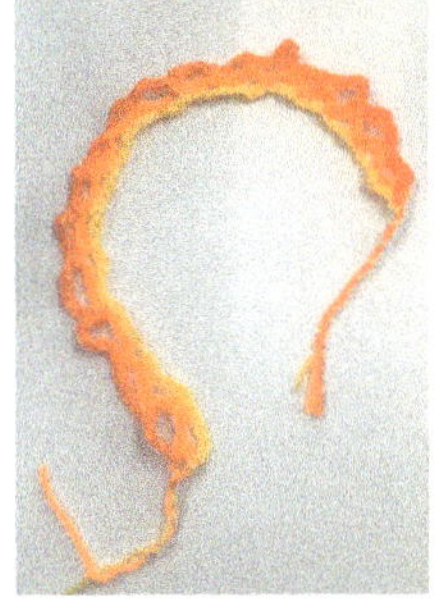
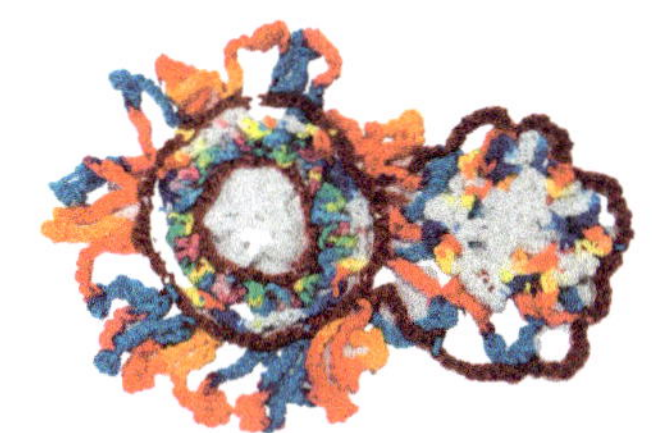
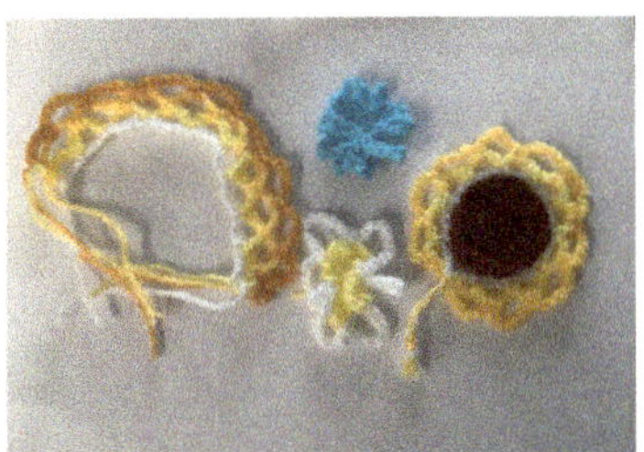
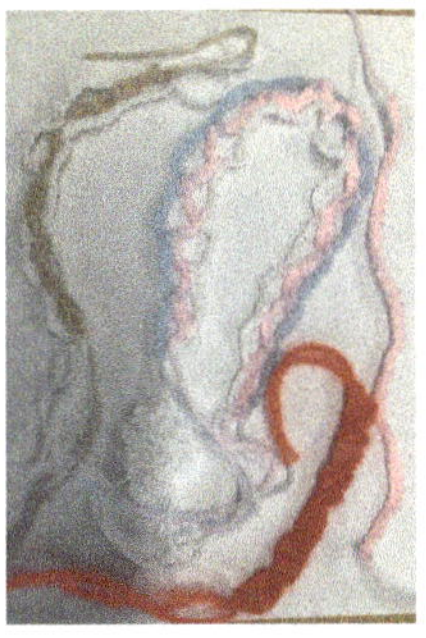
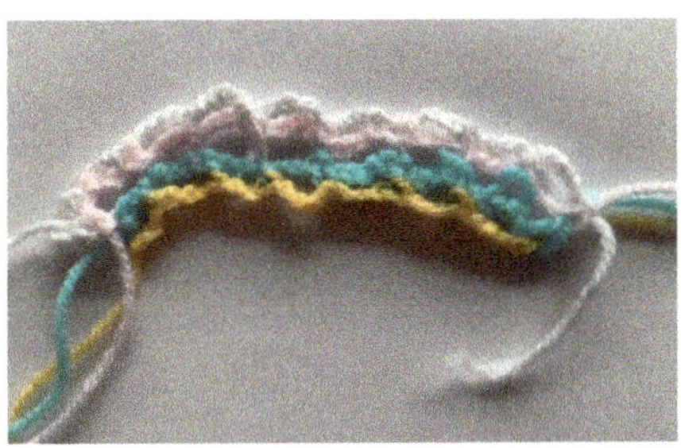

Headband

Work a foundation row which will fit over your head. It needs to be loose, depending on the yarn thickness. Choose rainbow coloured yarn or your own choice of colours. There is no fixed pattern for this and working freely comes with practice.

It is possible to join the yarn on the end of the work and work up to the top of the first loop, using a couple of slip stitches. To finish, make one chain at the end, pulling through all the coloured yarns at once.

It is important to stress, working loosely. If you begin with a tight chain it is quite difficult to work with.

The tension of the foundation row may cause the work to become slightly curved, which is why a headband is a good starting subject when creating a fabric.

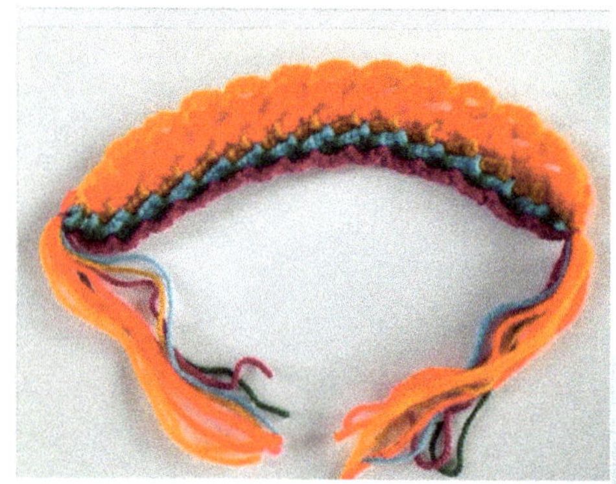

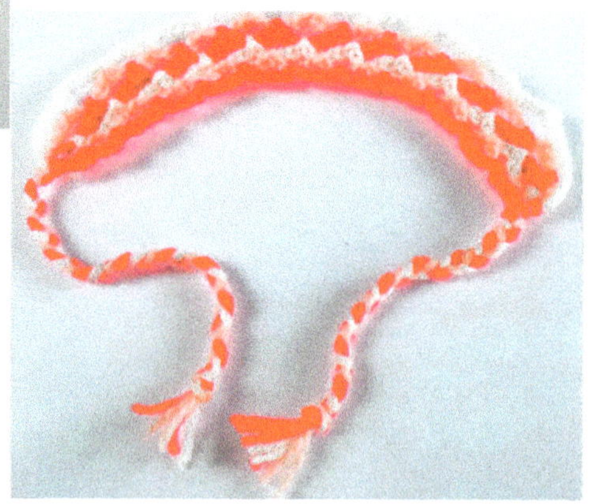

Making Flowers

The approach to Crochet Art, is very different from learning traditional crochet. It is only necessary to begin with two stitches, worked in the form of bridges and it is possible to use them creatively, as a medium for making fabric for pictures.

Similarly, the petals on flowers are like bridges because they can be formed, using chain and slip stitch too.

Using the idea of making flowers instead of rows, is a freeform approach to learning crochet.

Using a flower for a centre circle, is a great way to start making a fabric, which will grow in a circular fashion.

There are no patterns to follow and no mistakes, just experimental learning.

Comparatively, traditional crochet is learned, using a specific set of traditional, basic stitches and practiced in rows, with the emphasis on getting them straight.

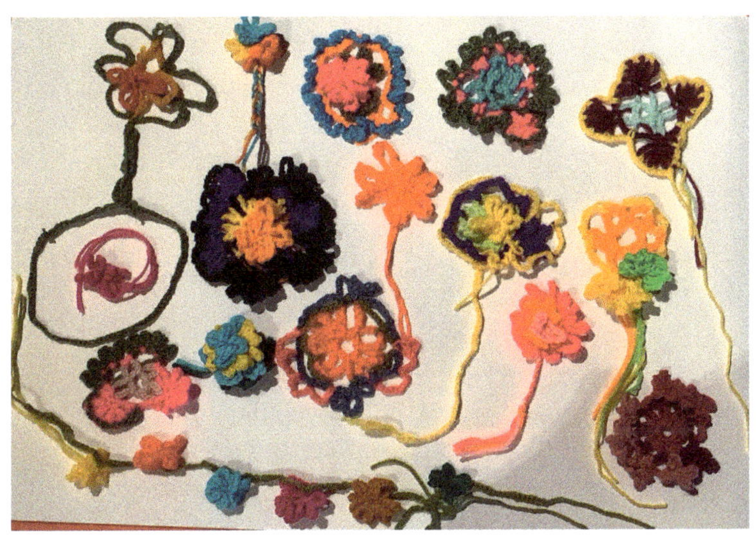

Squares

To begin 'painting with yarn', make some random patches to get a feel for how the colours and stitches can come together. It is easier to make rectangular patches than circular ones because you will need to increase the number of stitches around a circle, to keep it flat.

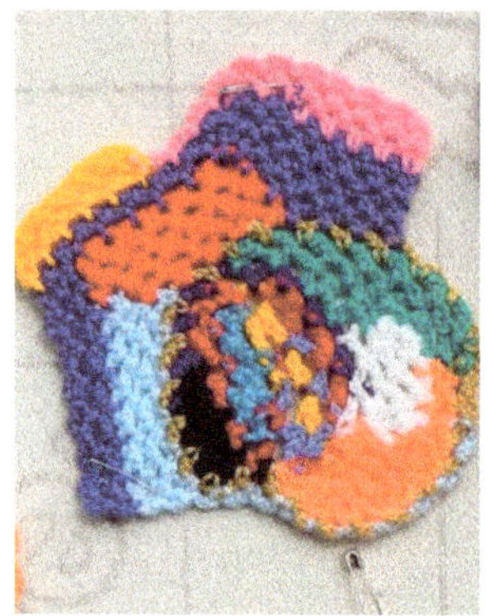

Begin by making something informal using different colours of dk yarn (double knit yarn).
Begin with a small chain length.

Next make a small square and work around the sides using different coloured yarns.

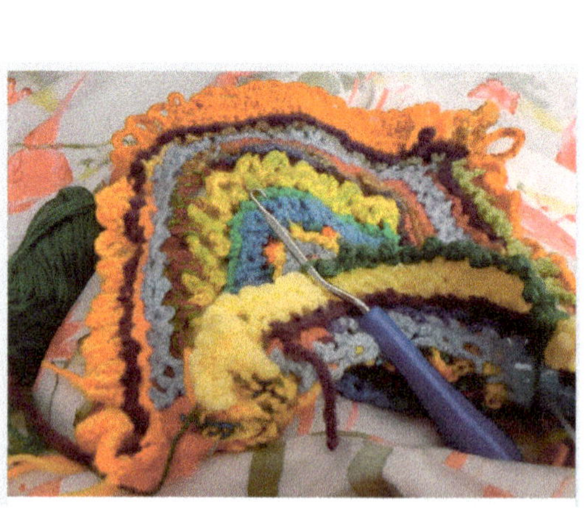

Making Fabric

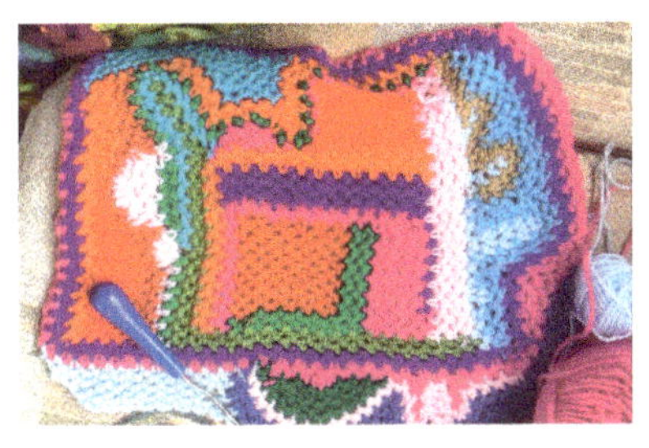

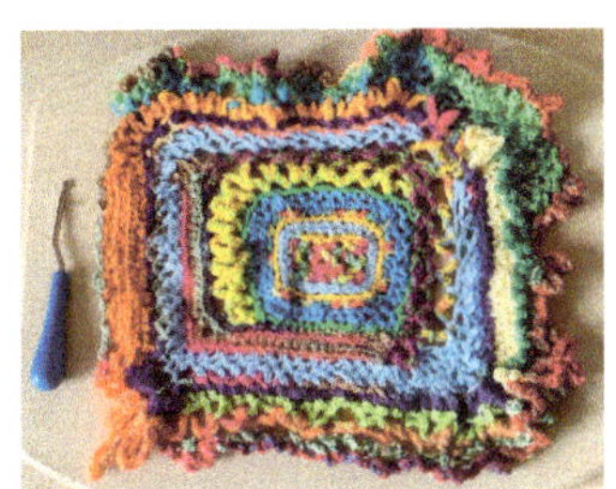

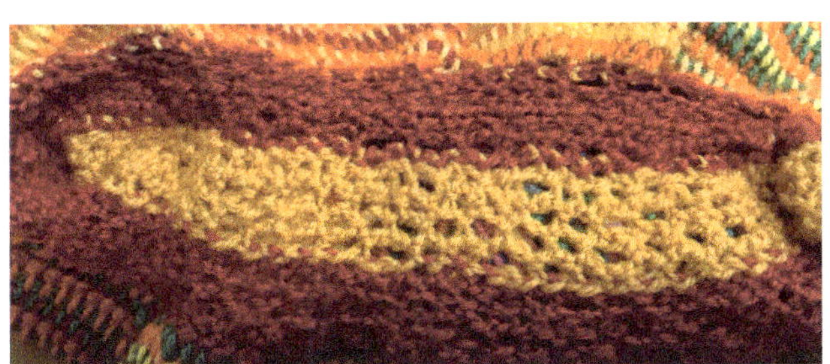

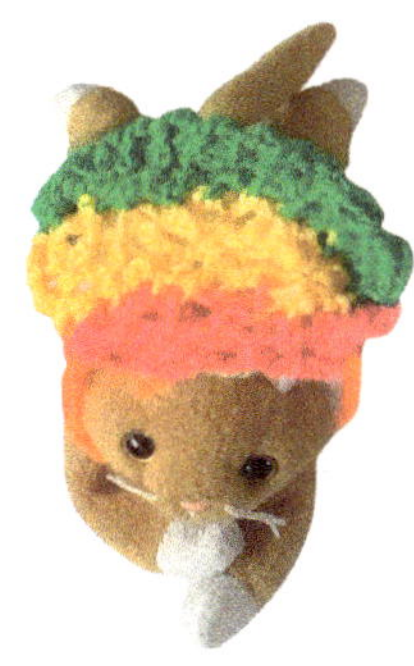

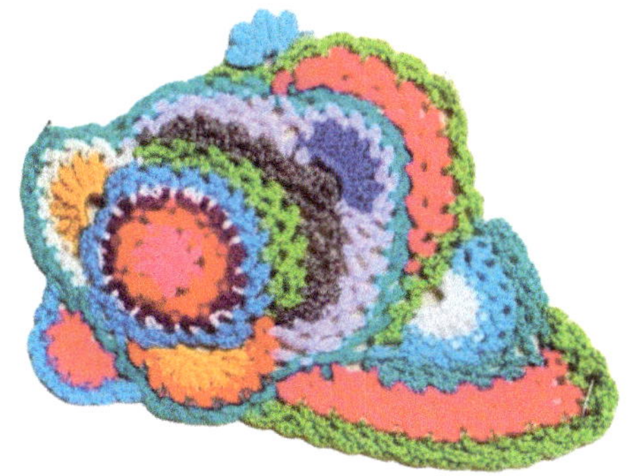

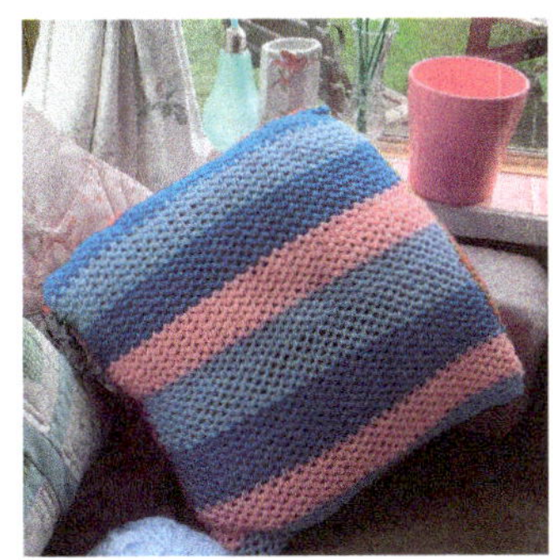

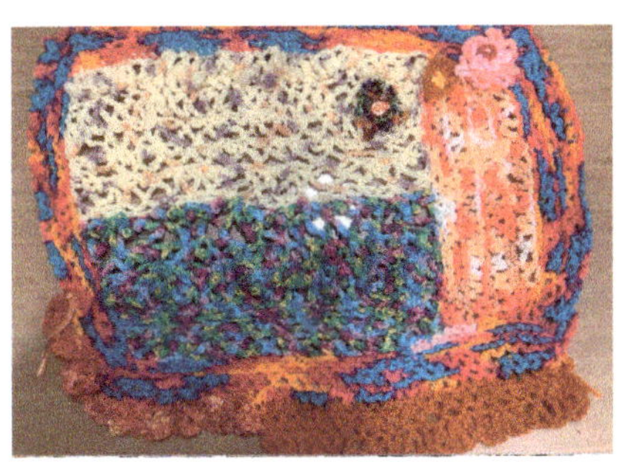

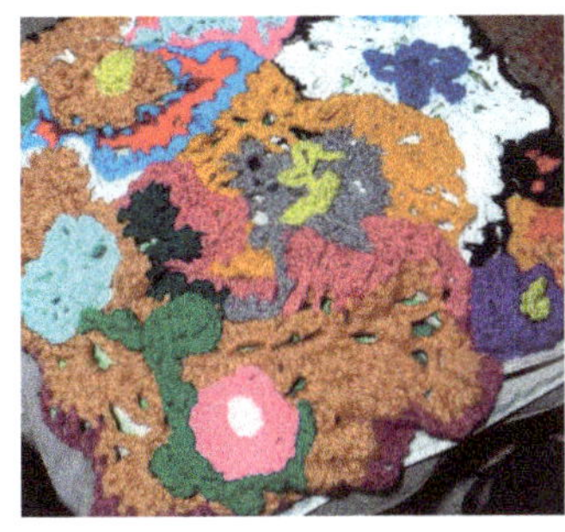

Circles

When making a circle, begin with a chain length of 3 chain stitches and hook into the first chain to make a small ring. Work around this ring using bridges of one chain stitch for the first round and two chain stitches for the next round. Then increase to 3 chain stitch bridges. You will find that without any further increases it will begin to curve upwards. To keep it flat you must start to gradually increase the number of bridges. To achieve this in a freeform manner it will take practice.

You will soon see it start to curve if you haven't increased enough.

You may increase, by making one or two bridges of 4 chains or make a bridge on top of a bridge in the previous row by hooking under a bridge twice.

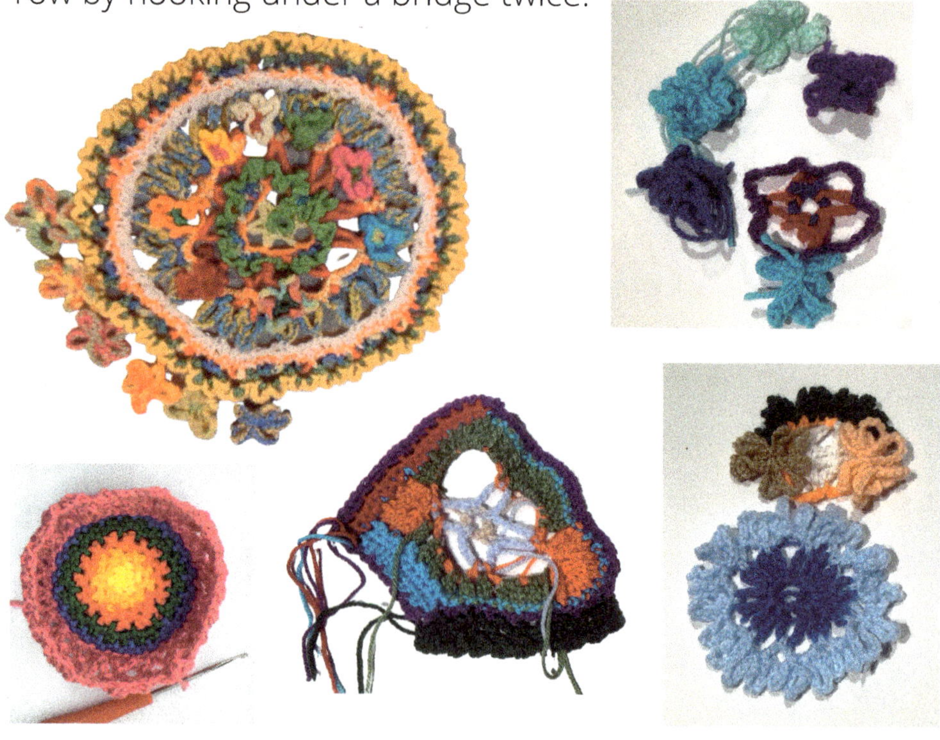

Making Pictures

When making a picture, begin with 'bridges' of 3 chain stitches.

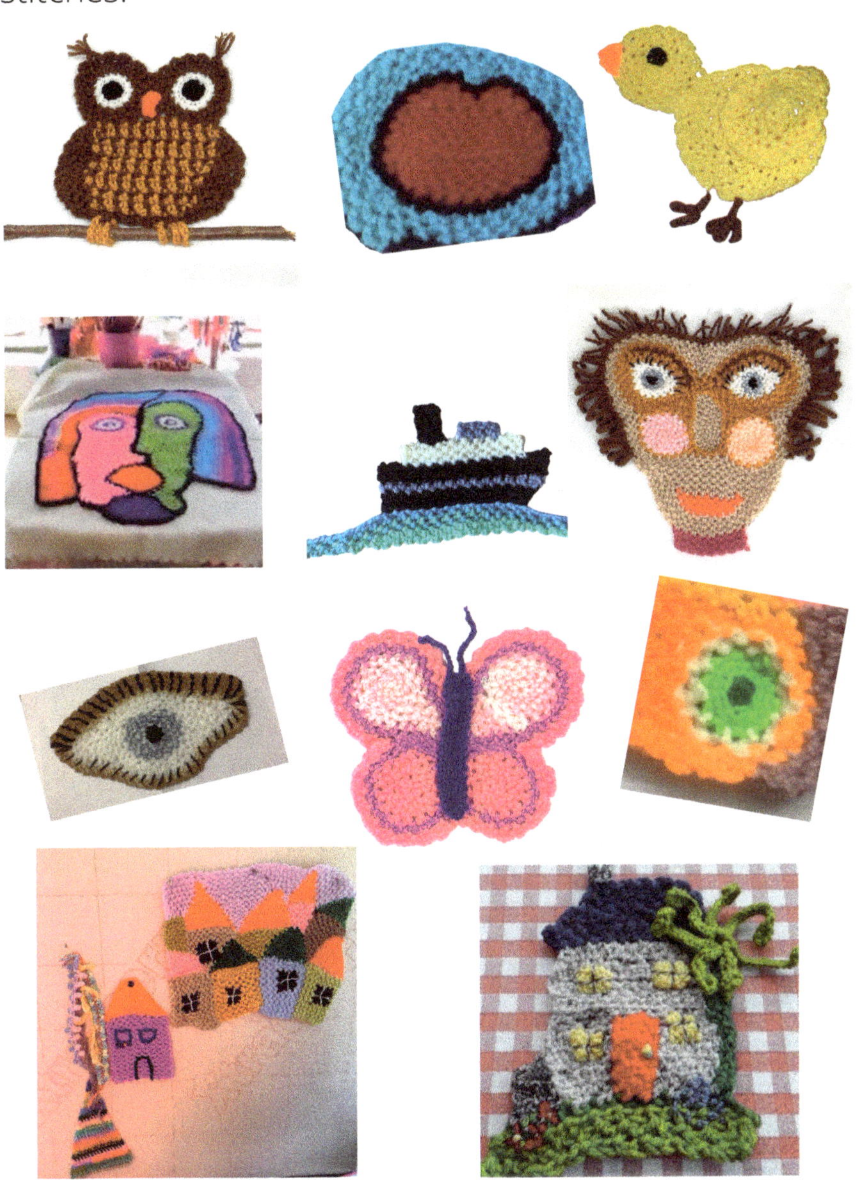

Making a face

Google 'face images' for ideas. Choose an image with large patches of colour. It's like drawing with yarn and because all the parts of the face can be any shape you want them to be, you can't get it wrong.

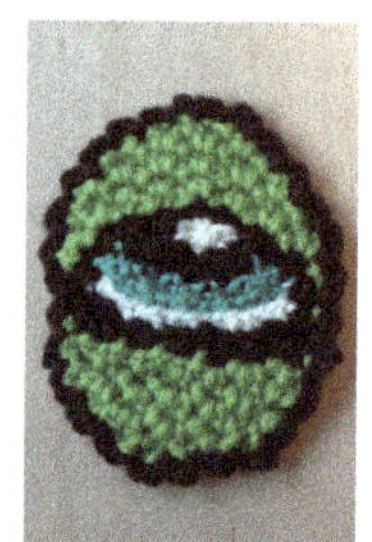

First make the eye,

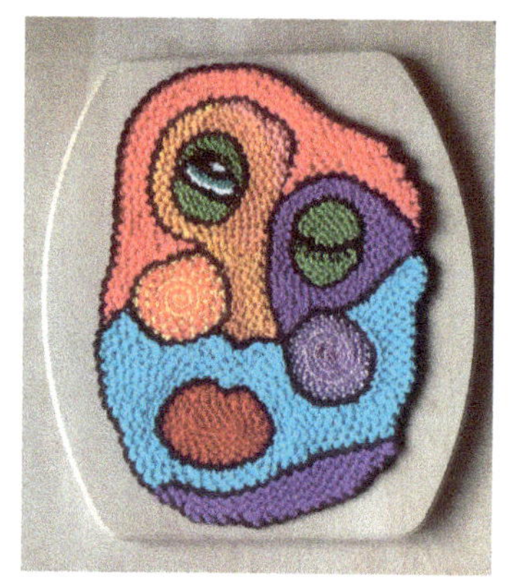

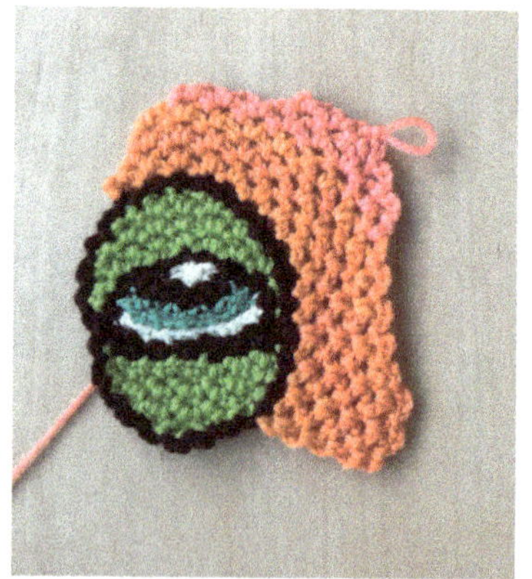

then begin working around the left eye

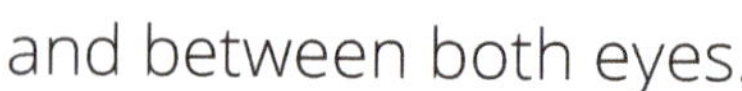

and between both eyes.

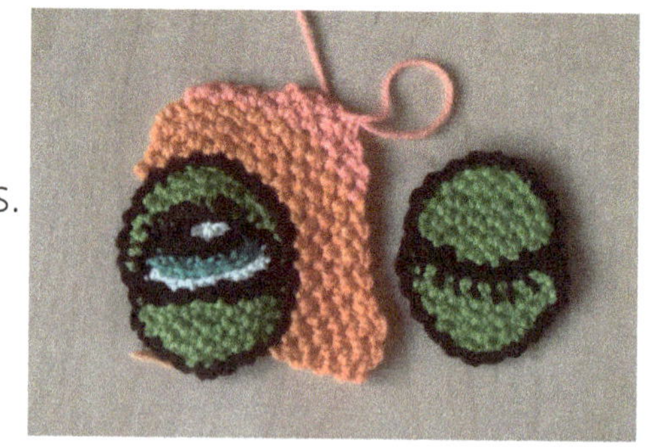

The Eyes

Eyes can be as simple or as complex as you want them. Type 'eye images' in your browser. Or try, 'eye drawing images' or even 'eye drawing cartoon images'. I have also researched animal and birds eyes this way.

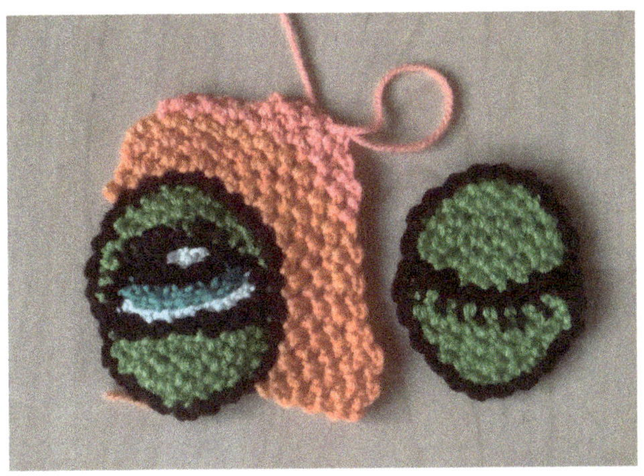

Making the eyes match is quite tricky. I opted for the closed eye because it was quicker, but I wondered if I would regret the quirkiness of it when finished. But then a beginner may like to go with the easier option of a sleeping face or even covering one eye with hair!

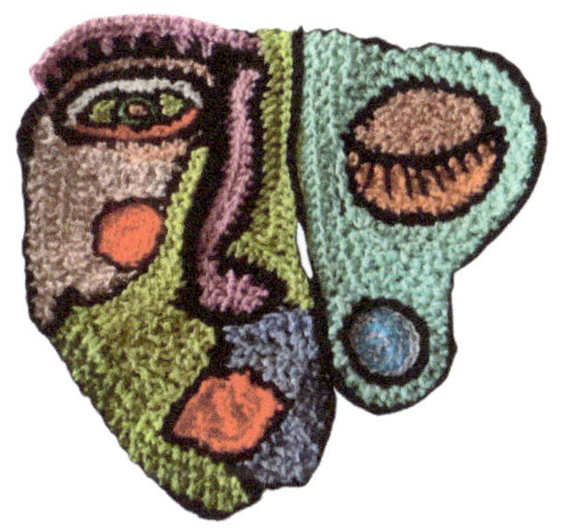

Cheeks

For the cheeks I used two spiral circles and if you are used to freeform crochet, you can make a similar design. However the easiest way is to make the cheeks a plain circle. It really doesn't matter if they are an irregular circle or an oval shape. In another face, I used two paisley shapes for cheeks, to fit in the face nicely like cheek bones. I like to add a black border around each element, to make them stand out but to make it simple, you don't have to do this. You may want to first sketch, how the pieces are going to look in position. The eyes, like mine, don't have to be in line. Move the elements around to wherever you want.

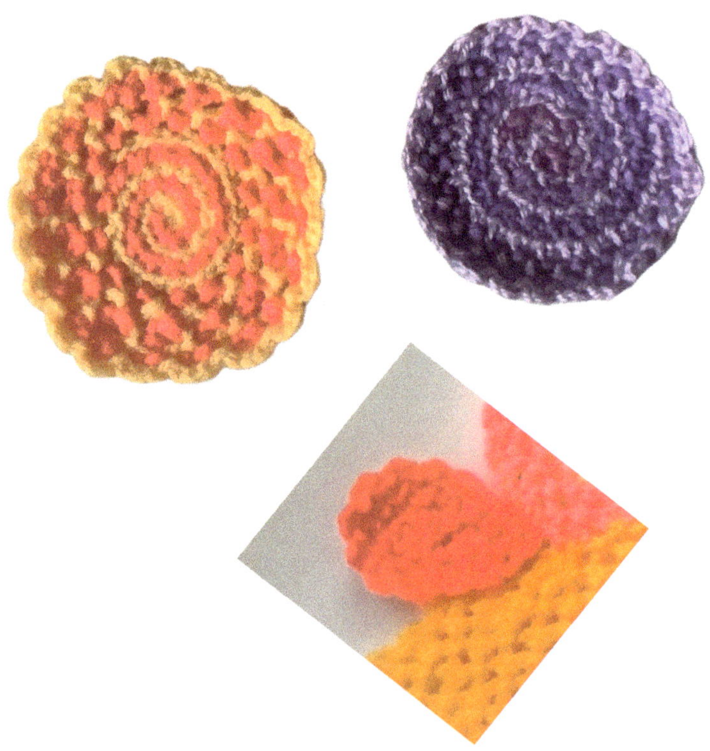

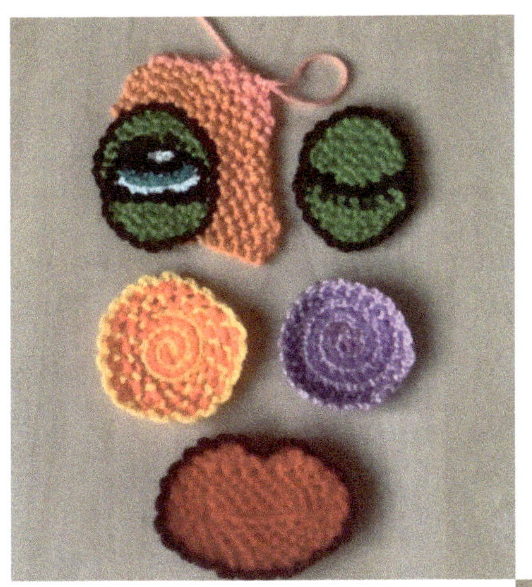

Mouth

and

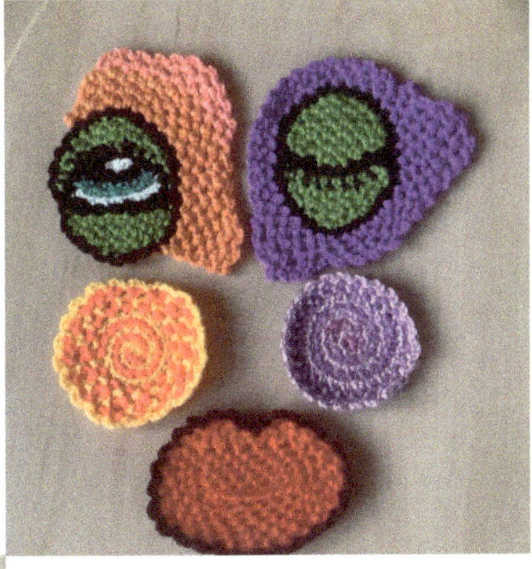

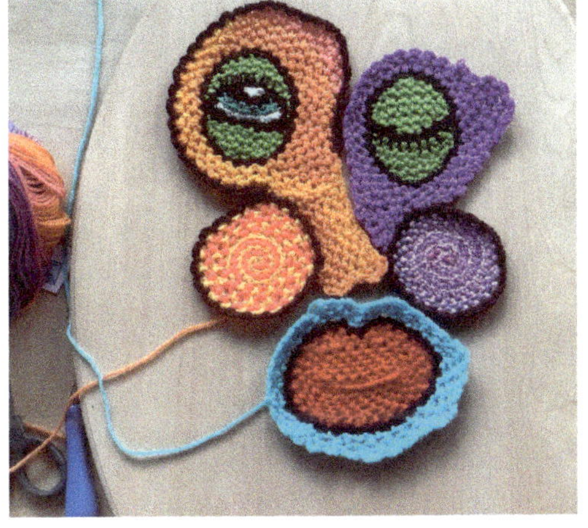

Nose

Mouth and Nose

Decide the general shape of the mouth and nose and where you would like them to go. You can work the nose as separate patch, or you can include it with one of the eyes as in my example.

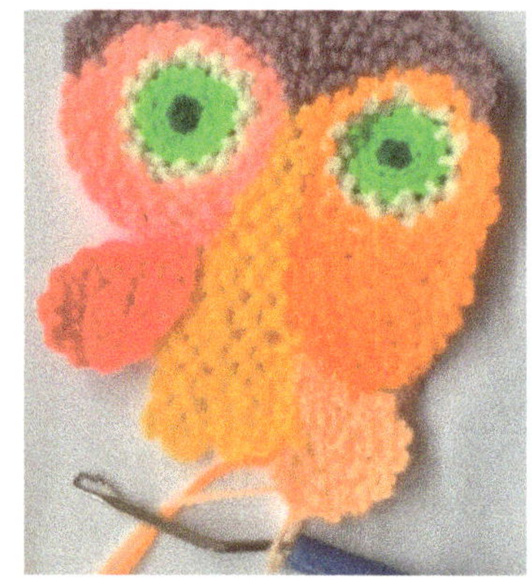

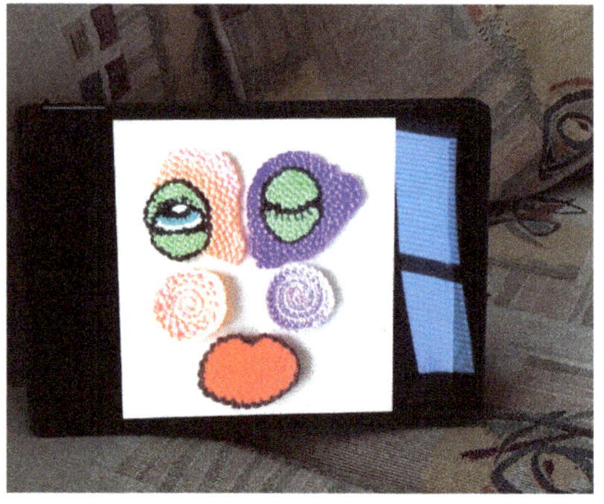

If you have access to a tablet, It may be helpful to view the work as a screen photo.

Now decide on the colours you want to fill in the rest of the face with. Begin by working around the outside of the eyes and also, the outside of the mouth. Make extra bridges or small loops, to add shape to the eyes and mouth. See the photograph and as you work, the shapes can be stitched where they meet.

If you simply go around the mouth, I found that it can become almost ape faced, so it's a good idea to extend to each side of the jaw, unless you would like it to be more animal like. I added a bottom line in purple, to give a shadow effect under the chin.

It is far better when making the face, to expect some freedom of design because it is not necessary to count the stitches and therefore there is no exact pattern to follow. You may even like to extend the face, to include hair, neck, shoulders, ears, hair adornments or jewellery. These can be added with freeform crochet or with embroidery.

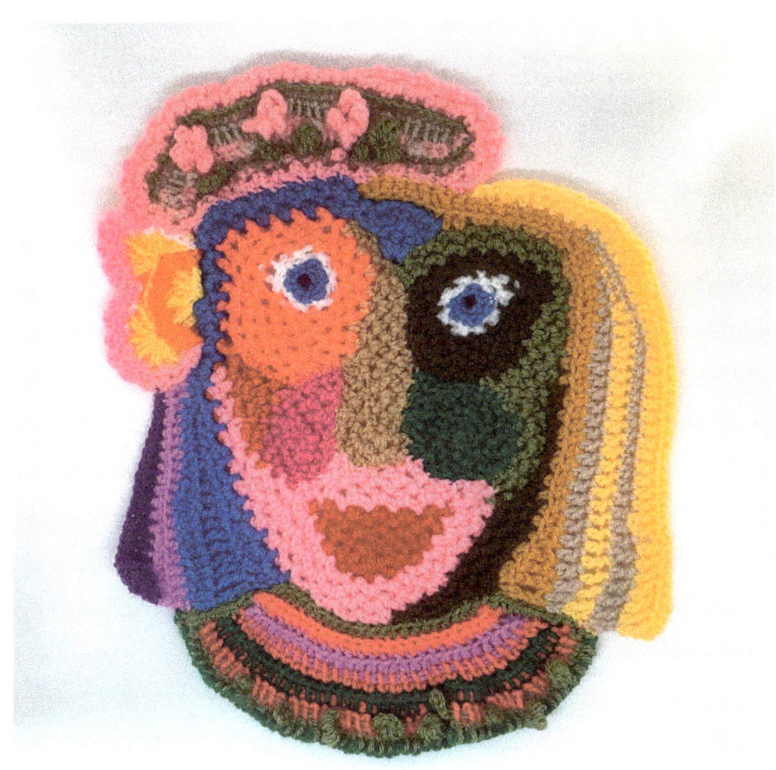

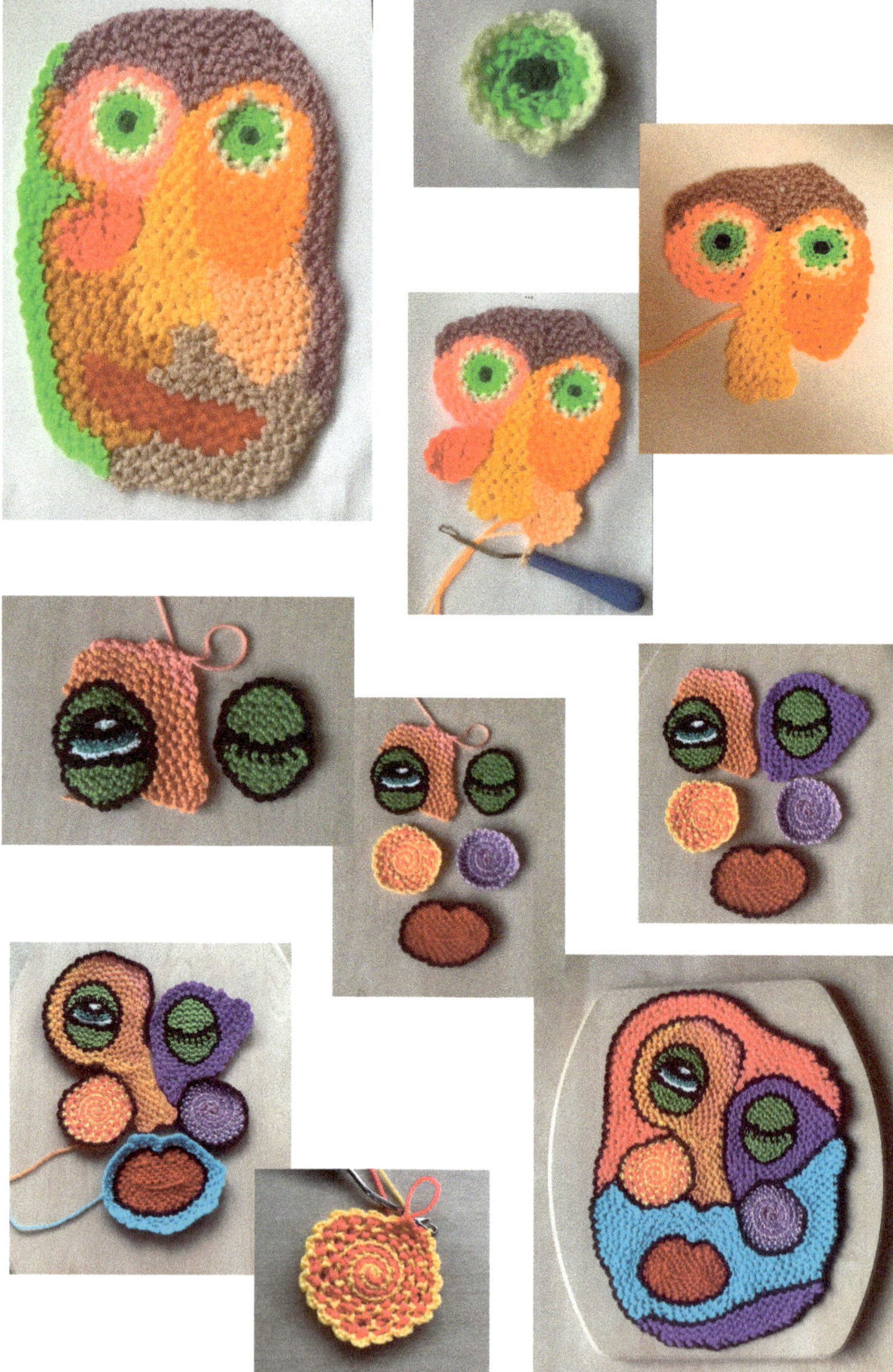

Have fun

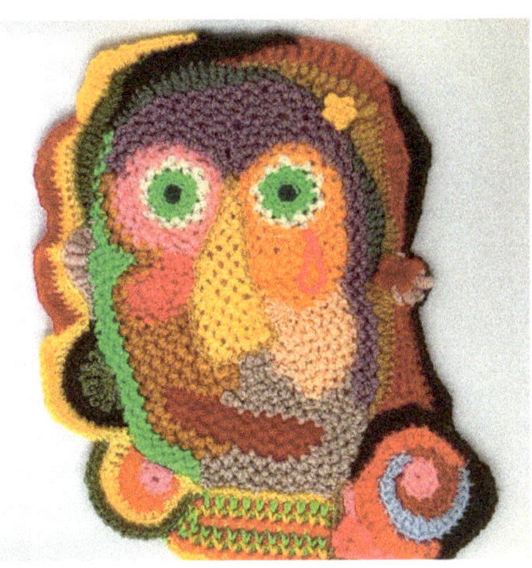

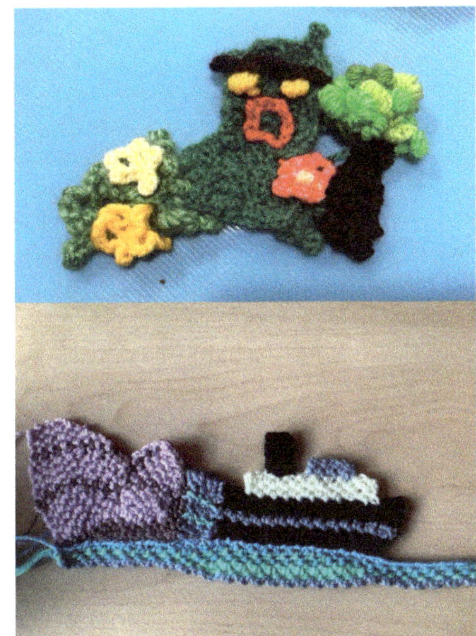

designing pictures and faces!

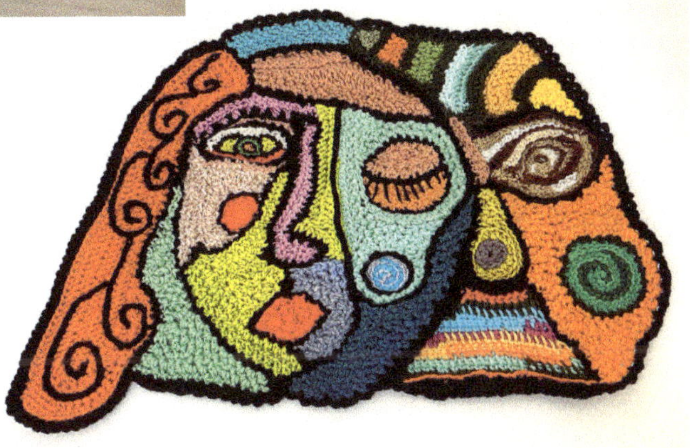

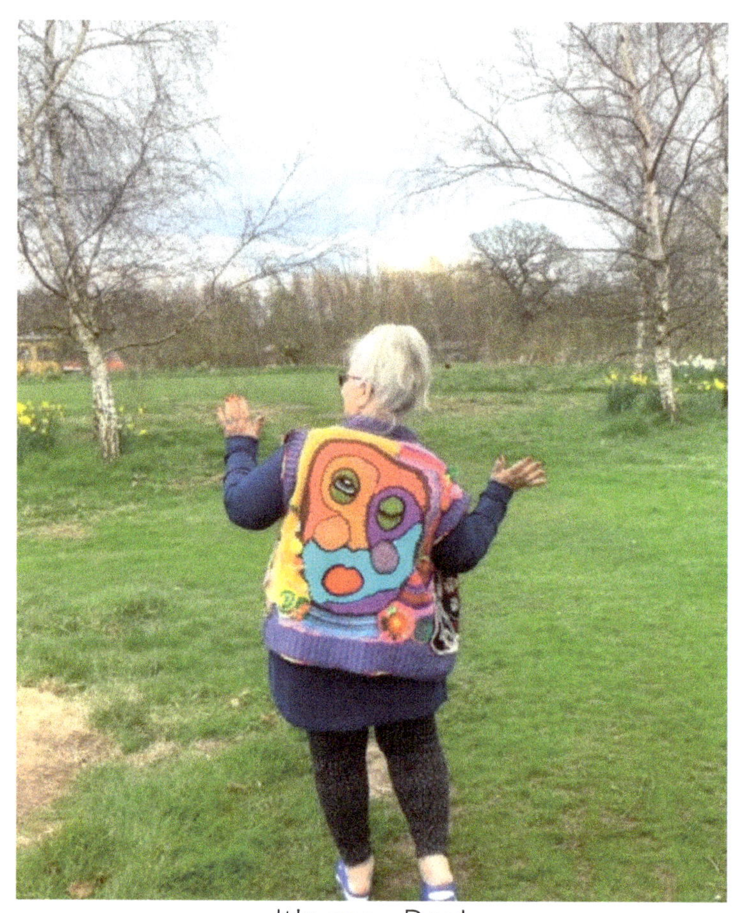

It's me...Roz!

If you have enjoyed this project then do join the facebook group 'Crochet Art' where you can post photos of your own face project. I would love to see them!
Please leave a review and subscribe to my YouTube channel.

Roslyn Hill

Acknowledgements

Please join my groups where you may post and share your crochet art with others:-
Facebook Page: Crochet the Easy Way
Facebook Group: Crochet Art
Blog: easycrochetblog.com
Email: 4321roz@gmail.com
Subscribe youtube.com/c/RoslynHillLatchHookCrochet

Author

Roslyn Hill B.Ed. studied as an art teacher and is a retired primary school teacher. Working with textiles has been her passion, including felting, quilting, weaving, tapestry, knitting, machine knitting, canvas work and crochet, including freeform crochet.

More recently, she is continually rethinking how crochet is taught, particularly with how children learn, finding new and easy ways to encourage teachers to include crochet in the classroom.

Latch Patch Publishing

www.ingramcontent.com/pod-product-compliance
Ingram Content Group UK Ltd.
Pitfield, Milton Keynes, MK11 3LW, UK
UKHW062300290726
14090UKWH00017B/800

9 781999 376543